GOD'S WORD. EVERY CHILD.

December 19, 2013

Dear Friend,

This is to say *thank you*. This Bible study guide is a gift of thanks from me and the OneHope team.

Your prayers and generosity make a tremendous difference. And because you're standing with OneHope to help present God's Word to every child and youth in the world, I know you have a deep respect and love for the Word. <u>I believe this study guide will help you immerse yourself in the great story of Scripture, from Genesis to Revelation.</u>

A dear pastor (and former OneHope missionary) friend of OneHope, along with his fellow associate pastor prepared the guide for us — to help you and your family dig into God's Word in the new year in a practical and engaging way. I pray you will enjoy it yourself, or pass it along to a friend.

I know you believe, as I do, that God's Word transforms. "For the Word of God is alive and active. Sharper than any double-edged sword ..." (Hebrews 4:12). It was this powerful Word that transformed a 14-year-old Hindu boy named Ria ...

Ria was struggling with many questions about his life and future. The gods and goddesses of his traditional religion offered no help. But when the *Book of Hope* arrived at his school, everything changed. <u>Ria discovered the love of the one true God, and chose to follow Him.</u>

Thank you for reaching out to young people like Ria, all over the world, with the Good News. Your partnership is making a life-changing difference!

Your partner in world missions,

Rob

Rob Hoskins

600 SW 3rd Street, Pompano Beach, FL 33060 • Phone: 800.448.2425 ~ 954.975.7777 • Fax: 954.975.0620
www.onehope.net

BY CRAIG BELLISARIO

& BRIAN MINNICH

WORD

IN THE

GOD'S STORY
REVEALED

This is love: not that we loved God, but that he loved us and sent his Son as an atoning sacrifice for our sins.

— 1 John 4:10 (NIV)

A WORD ABOUT ONEHOPE

Founded in 1987, OneHope is an international ministry that is changing lives by sharing Scripture with young people around the world. Each Scripture program is age-specific and customized based on research OneHope conducts among children and youth, leaders and educators in the countries it works. In collaboration with churches and ministries — and working with local governments, schools and non-governmental organizations — OneHope has reached nearly a billion young people in more than 125 countries with a relevant Gospel message. Our mission: *to affect destiny by providing God's eternal Word to all the children and youth of the world.* Our name reflects our desire to present the Living Word of God to children and youth in an engaging way. Jesus Christ is the one and only hope for eternity — and when we present Him to the next generation lives are transformed.

TABLE OF CONTENTS

FORWARD

How do you feel about reading the Bible?

This is a foundational question for those of us who long to engage with God's Word in a relevant way ... but it is a question many followers of Christ grapple with. If we find we are not consistently reading all of the Bible ... why aren't we?

Perhaps it's the age-old question of *Where do I start?* "In the beginning," with Genesis, working your way to the end, as with any other book? Or maybe you take the "close your eyes, open your Bible, and point" approach. Perhaps you outsource the decision, using a devotional book to help you figure it out — whatever verses are listed under today's date, that's where you're headed.

Or maybe your frustration comes after you've begun reading. Things start out okay, but then you hit a brick wall. *What does this passage mean? How does this apply to my life? What did I just read?*

Parts of the Bible can honestly seem confusing, even to devoted Christians. We may find ourselves wondering, *Are these just random stories and ideas, with only the slimmest common thread? How do these stories and ideas connect with each other? What does Leviticus have to do with my relationship with Jesus — or my daily life?*

If you've ever asked yourself these questions, you're not alone.

And, I have some good news for you: There *is* a purpose in every book of the Bible. It *is* organized. And you *can* understand it.

In fact, God wants you to be able to read His Word and comprehend "the words of eternal life" He has to share with you (John 6:68).

This book is designed to help you and your family understand the meta-narrative of Scripture — God's big picture.

As you follow this guide throughout the year, you'll begin to see the connections among all of those stories that may have seemed "random" before ... You'll discover how every single one of them relates to the ultimate and incredible plan God made for you from the very beginning.

By this time next year, I trust you'll be able to look at your Bible with new clarity, insight, and understanding. You'll know, better than ever, where to look for the biblical wisdom and encouragement you need. Plus, strengthening the foundation of your Bible knowledge will help you to grow in your relationship with God!

May God bless you!

— Rob Hoskins,
President of OneHope
December 2013

INTRODUCTION

Shortly into my first year as a pastor, a young woman in her 20's approached me and said, "I hear what you are saying and I am reading my Bible, but I just don't understand what I am reading." Realizing her dilemma was shared by many others, Craig and I put together a read-through-the-Bible study for our congregation. The goal is for God's people to engage God's Word with understanding. Some questions are designed to bring understanding of God's character and plan for his people, and other questions cause us to reflect and apply God's Word to our lives. We are thrilled to partner with OneHope in this project and pray God will enrich you this year by his Word.

— Brian Minnich

BIBLE IN A YEAR

Month	Topic Title	Entire Scripture	Main Theme	Main Characters	Events
January	Creation	Genesis 1 – 11	God creates man but sin enters the world	Adam, Noah	Creation, Fall, Flood, Babel
January	Patriarchs	Genesis 12 – 50	God chooses Abraham to father a nation to represent God to the world	Abraham, Isaac, Jacob, Joseph	Abraham's Journey, Isaac and Jacob, Joseph in Egypt
February	Exodus	Exodus – Deuteronomy	God delivers His people and gives them the Law	Moses	Deliverance, The Law, The People Rebel, Forty Years of Wandering
March	Promised Land	Joshua	God's people subdue the Promised Land by faith	Joshua	Jordan, Jericho, Conquering the Land, Dominion of Land
April	Judges	Judges – Ruth	Judges are chosen to lead the people over 400 years	Deborah, Samson, Gideon, Ruth	Deborah, Samson, Gideon, Ruth
May	Kingdom	1 Samuel – 2 Chronicles	Israel becomes a Kingdom, faces judgment for its sin, and is sent into exile	Samuel, Saul, David, Solomon	Samuel and Saul, David, Solomon, Kingdoms of Israel
June	Exile and Return	Ezekiel, Daniel, Ezra, Nehemiah, Esther	Israel is exiled for 70 years then led back to rebuild Jerusalem	Daniel, Ezra, Nehemiah, Esther	Exile, Return of the Exiled, Nehemiah Rebuilds the Wall, Esther
July	The Prophets	Isaiah – Malachi	God uses the prophets to proclaim His Word for both the future and the present	The Prophets	See the general description of each book
August	Poetical	Job – Song of Songs	God's message is communicated poetically through a number of different literary techniques	Job, David, Solomon	Job; Psalms; Proverbs; Ecclesiastes and Song of Songs
September	Christ on Earth	Matthew – John	Jesus comes and offers salvation through His death and resurrection.	Jesus, The Disciples	Pre-Ministry, Public Ministry, Ministry to the Disciples, Death and Resurrection
October	Church and Growth	Acts	God establishes and expands the Church through the obedience of His followers	Peter, Paul	Birth of the Church, Church Growth and Persecution, Paul's Missionary Journeys, Paul's Imprisonment
November	Pauline Epistles	Romans – Philemon	Paul's letters to encourage and instruct in the Christian faith	Paul, as the only author	See the general description of each book
December	General Epistles	Hebrews – Revelation	Letters from early Christian leaders to encourage and instruct in the faith	Jesus	See the general description of each book

STUDY OVERVIEW

Goals

1. To understand and see the Bible as a continuous story, not a bunch of random books.
2. To see God's salvation plan for man at work throughout the Bible.
3. To learn how to study the Bible.
4. To develop good Bible reading habits.
5. To engage with God's Word in a greater way.

Format

Every month will cover a different section of the Bible, further broken down into four weekly assignments.

CREATION & PATRIARCHS

Creation

"Once upon a time ..."

Familiar words. Your parents probably read fairy tales to you with this famous opening line, and you may have even shared those same stories with your own children and grandchildren since then.

Though all fairy tales basically start with the same phrase, it's from these first words that an incredible story takes on a life of its own.

Soon, a setting is formed — the woods, a small town, a far-off land. Heroes and villains are introduced. A dilemma is presented to the gallant main character. Obstacles are overcome, challenges are faced.

Then the climax — the good guy and the bad guy square off for the final battle. Just as the curtain of defeat seems to make its descent, the hero comes through. Victory!

With this triumph, all is set right in the land. The hero gets the girl, the enemy is vanquished, peace replaces conflict, and "they all lived Happily Ever After."

These fairy tales are not unlike the story we read in the Bible, with one key exception: The Bible is TRUE!

> **Fairy tales are not unlike the story we read in the Bible, with one key exception: The Bible is TRUE!**

Every account we read in Scripture is God-ordained,[2] and tells the true story of humanity.

From the first words in Genesis 1:1 ... "In the beginning God created the heavens and the earth" ... the story unfolds. And, as these first words illustrate, it's a story about God and His creation.

Once the setting is formed — literally, Earth is formed — God, Satan, and many other heroic and villainous characters are introduced. It doesn't take long for the problem of sin to show up, threatening to eternally separate creation (that's us!) from God. So God works out a plan to reunite us with Him.

And the plan is carried out, climaxing at the cross where it seems like death has won. But at the last minute, our hero Jesus rises from the dead, alive and triumphant!

All is set right on Earth. Jesus gets His bride (that's us again!), Satan and death are defeated, peace returns to the land, and we all live "Happily Ever After" with Christ for eternity.

It's an incredible, supernatural story ... God's ultimate love story, and we're the ones He's in love with. And it all begins right here in Genesis.

> **Scripture Coverage:** Genesis 1 – 11
> **Scripture Reading:** Genesis 1 – 11
> **Book Genre:** Historical
> **Main Theme:** God creates man, but sin enters the world.
> **Main Events:** Creation, Fall, Flood, Babel
> **Main Characters:** Adam, Noah

Week 1: Creation
Scripture: Genesis 1 – 2

1. What does it mean when God says He created man in His own image? (Genesis 1:27)

2. What attributes of God (His character, qualities, traits) do you see in the Creation story?

3. Why does God put Adam in the Garden of Eden? (Genesis 2:15)

4. What is the one thing God commands Adam not to do? (Genesis 2:16)

5. What institution does God establish between a man and a woman? Is this contradictory to what is practiced in today's society?

6. Why are you, as a person, more special in God's sight than other parts of His creation?

7. How does it make you feel to know that God created you? How might you want to live your life in light of this knowledge?

Week 1: Fall
Scripture: Genesis 3

1. Who is the serpent? What is implied by the question he asks? (Genesis 3:1)

2. What tactic does the serpent use to tempt the woman into eating from the tree in the middle of the garden? How are you similarly tempted? What can you learn from this exchange about "resist[ing] the devil"? (Genesis 3:4-5; James 4:7)

_____

_____

_____

3. From this account, how could you define sin?

_____

_____

_____

4. What can you learn about the consequences of sin, specifically and in general?

_____

_____

_____

5. In the midst of the judgment, the goodness of God shines through. Sometimes called the "protevangelium"[3] or pre-gospel, the first announcement of a coming Messiah and the work of redemption provides hope. What promise does God make, and what similarities do you see between this promise and the life of Jesus? (Genesis 3:15)

_____

_____

_____

6. What temptations are you facing right now? What does God promise about help in times of struggle? (1 Corinthians 10:13)

_____

_____

_____

7. The righteousness of God requires a judgment on sin — death. But, because of God's great love for us, He has provided His Son to die in our place. Think about

where you would be without God's love and sacrifice. Give Him glory and thanks in your own way.

_____

_____

_____

Week 2: Flood
Scripture: Genesis 6 – 9

1. Why does God send the Flood? (Genesis 6:5-6)

_____

_____

_____

2. What kind of person is Noah?

_____

_____

_____

3. The Bible says "Faith without works is dead." Noah shows his faith by doing everything the Lord asked of him. Does the way you live your life reflect your belief in God? What evidence of your faith do you see in your life? (James 2:20; Genesis 5:22)

_____

_____

_____

4. What area(s) of your life do you need to surrender to God? It could be finances, service to others, a relationship, or something else that you know is not pleasing to the Lord. What steps can you take to show your faith through obedience?

_____

_____

_____

5. Noah doesn't hear from God for at least 150 days. Put yourself in Noah's place — how might you feel living in the ark for that long with no direction from God? (Genesis 7:24) In the middle of this great catastrophe, God is silent. How do you feel when you go through trials and God doesn't speak? Why do you think God gets quiet sometimes?

6. What comfort can we take from Genesis 8:1?

7. Noah and his family eventually make it through the Flood by relying on God. God often brings people through flood waters to teach dependence on Him. What struggles are you facing now that require God's power to overcome? Pray for God to strengthen your endurance and faith.

Week 2: Babel
Scripture: Genesis 11

1. What is the world like as the Tower of Babel is being built? (Genesis 11:1-4)

2. What is man's plan? What two-fold purpose do the people have in doing this?

3. How does this plan fly directly in the face of God's previous commandment to mankind? (Genesis 9:1)

4. What comfort might people draw from staying in one place? Is it scary for you to leave what is known or familiar? What lesson might God have been teaching man in this example? How can you learn from it, too?

5. What does God do to thwart man's plan? What origin might be explained by this event in Scripture?

6. What is the final result of God's confusing the languages of the people?

Patriarchs[4]

"You can choose your friends, but you can't choose your family."

The old adage is true. When you were born, you didn't get to choose who your mom and dad would be. There was no election process. You just arrived, and you were theirs.

Consequently, you didn't have a say in who your siblings, aunts, uncles, cousins, nieces, nephews, or grandparents would be. The people you bump into at family reunions or travel cross-country to visit ... the people who visit your home or even live across the hall from you ... weren't hand-selected like a peach in the produce aisle. When it comes to family, for better or worse — bruises and all — you're stuck with them.

God begins His work of redemption by choosing a people to reflect and represent Himself to the world.

Throughout the rest of Genesis, you're going to read about a family. In their story, you will see moments of passion, love, and sacrifice. Some will literally lay down their lives for one another. But this family, like many families, is also dysfunctional — acts of betrayal, deception, and violence abound.

All this from one family. You might know them as God's "chosen people."

God begins His work of redemption by choosing a people to reflect and represent Himself to the world. With this goal in mind, He called Abraham (originally Abram, but renamed by God to reflect His purpose for Abraham as "father of many").

A covenant is established between God and Abraham — a man the Lord set aside for Himself, who will be separate from the world and worship the One True God. And this lineage will travel from Abraham to Isaac, from Isaac to Jacob, from Jacob to his twelve sons — from whom the twelve tribes of Israel will be named.

As you read, you'll be amazed by God's faithfulness in dealing with this family, full of imperfect people. You might also learn more than you bargained for — about interacting with your own flawed family, and becoming a righteous servant of God!

> **Scripture Coverage:** Genesis 12 - 50
> **Scripture Reading:** Genesis 12 - 50
> **Book Genre:** Historical
> **Main Theme:** God chooses Abraham to father a nation that will demonstrate how God relates to His creation.
> **Main Events:** Abraham's Journey, Isaac and Jacob, Joseph in Egypt
> **Main Characters:** Abraham, Isaac, Jacob, Joseph

Week 3: Abraham's Journey
Scripture: Genesis 12 – 25

1. What commandment and promises does God give to Abram? (Genesis 12:1-3)

2. The promise that "all peoples on earth will be blessed through [Abram]" is repeated in Genesis four other times. In light of God's plan to bring about redemption for mankind, describe this promise and how God specifically brings it to pass. (Genesis 12:3; 18:18; 22:18; 28:14)

3. In Genesis, Abram uses deception to protect himself twice in Egypt. What does this tell us about Abram's faith and relationship with God at this point? Can you relate? (Genesis 12:10-20; 20)

4. God has promised Abram offspring, and even confirmed it. How does Abram try to "help" God? Have you ever tried to "help" God? (Genesis 15 – 16)

5. Abram's action causes serious family troubles. Sometimes trying to force things to happen rather than waiting on God makes the situation worse. What situations are you facing that require patience for God's timing?

6. God proves His faithfulness with the birth of Isaac. If Abraham had his way, it probably would have happened much sooner. Why did God wait so long to bring Isaac? What can we learn about God's timetable? (Genesis 21)

7. God makes what seems like a pretty horrific request from Abraham, but it shows just how far Abraham's relationship with the Lord has grown. Explain how Abraham has grown since his first steps with the Lord. How do you see similar steps of growth in your own journey with God? (Genesis 22)

8. Isaac is often referred to as a "type" of Christ, which means God used him and his situation to depict what would one day be fulfilled in the ministry of Jesus. What similarities do you see between Isaac and Jesus?

Week 4: Isaac and Jacob
Scripture: Genesis 21 - 36

1. What instances of God's providence[5] do you see in Abraham's servant finding Rebekah for Isaac? Think about an instance from your own past in which you can now see the hand of God at work. (Genesis 24)

2. What behavior(s) does Isaac display that remind you of Abraham? What does this tell you about the influence of a father? If you are a parent, what can you learn about the impact your life has on your children? (Genesis 26)

3. Like Abraham and Isaac, Jacob uses deception to manipulate circumstances in his favor. Share two instances in which you see Jacob acting deceptively.

4. Meeting with God can change a person. After Jacob wrestles with God, his name is changed to Israel. This is symbolic of a deeper change — he is a different person. No longer is he "the deceiver." Now, he is "one who struggles with God." Knowing this, what practical steps can you take to spend more time with God? Follow through on at least one of those steps now. (Genesis 32)

Week 4: Joseph in Egypt
Scripture: Genesis 37 – 50

1. Describe the circumstances that lead Joseph to Egypt. (Genesis 37)

2. Joseph faces the temptation to commit adultery with Potiphar's wife, but he doesn't give in. How was Joseph able to resist temptation? (Genesis 39)

3. Joseph has spent time in slavery and been wrongfully imprisoned for years. How would you feel if you were in Joseph's place? How does Joseph conduct himself as a slave? As a prisoner? What can we learn from his example?

4. Joseph recognizes God's hand (providence) in his life. Beyond saving the lives of Joseph's family, what is God doing in the grand scheme of things? (This relates to why God called this family to Himself.)

5. Describe the events of Genesis, from Creation to the death of Joseph. Be sure to include all the key events as outlined in the one-year grid.

Monthly Reflection

How did this month's study help you ...

1. Understand the Bible as a continuous story?

2. See God's salvation plan for man?

3. Learn how to study the Bible?

4. Grow in your personal walk with Jesus?

EXODUS

Exodus[6]

You see it in the news more and more often.

Hurricanes put coastal communities under water. Wildfires leave behind charred paths of destruction. Tornadoes lift homes off of foundations and send them careening back to earth in pieces. Earthquakes, tsunamis, and countless other natural disasters spring up with little or no warning ... and leave lives forever changed.

You don't even have to live in these devastated communities to see the impact. Go online or flip on the television, and pictures and videos are being posted or broadcast in real time —

Billions of dollars in property damage. Homes lost, businesses destroyed. Countless injured, missing, or dead.

It takes something pretty powerful to cause this kind of wreckage — whether gale-force winds or inferno-like temperatures.

But the Book of Exodus details an even stronger Power — our omnipotent[7] God.

> **You'll continue to see the Father's plan of redemption at work in the lives of His people — no longer a small family, but an entire nation!**

When His chosen people are in bondage, God works through Moses to unleash powerful plagues on the Egyptians — plagues that would make the natural disasters on the news today look like child's play.

And then, when the Israelites are finally free in the Great Exodus, God demonstrates His sovereignty once again by sustaining over one million people as they travel across the desert.

Plus, you'll continue to see the Father's plan for redemption at work in the lives of His people — no longer a small family, but an entire nation! Both God's love and His law are on full display, as He provides and protects while requiring obedience at the same time.

Though man's fear and lack of faith causes some setbacks — an entire generation misses out on the Promised Land — God is faithful. As you will see, nothing will hinder His plan.

> **Scripture Coverage:** Exodus – Deuteronomy
> **Scripture Reading:** Exodus 1 – 20; Numbers 11 – 14; Numbers 20 – 25; Deuteronomy 31 – 34
> **Book Genre:** Historical
> **Main Theme:** God delivers His people and gives them the Law[8]
> **Main Events:** Deliverance; The Law; The People Rebel; Forty Years of Wandering
> **Main Characters:** Moses

Week 1: Deliverance
Scripture: Exodus 1 – 18

1. Describe the events that lead the nation of Israel to be placed in bondage. (Exodus 1)

2. Describe the circumstances around the birth of Moses and what leads him to flee Egypt. (Exodus 1:15-2:15)

3. Much can be learned from Moses' conversation with God. What practical lesson(s) do you see in this passage? What does God tell Moses to do? How can you apply it to your life? (Exodus 3 – 4)

4. God uses various plagues to show His power to the Egyptians. After each plague, the Bible references Pharaoh's heart. What is happening to Pharaoh? What does it

mean to have a hardened heart? (Exodus 7 – 11)

5. In the final plague, all of the firstborn sons are killed, but the Israelites are spared because of their obedience to God's Passover instructions. What must the Israelites do to keep their homes safe? (Exodus 12)

6. The Passover points to what Jesus will one day do on the cross. Describe the similarities between the Passover lamb and Jesus, "the Lamb of God."

7. Pharaoh finally lets the people go, beginning the Exodus from Egypt into the Promised Land. This is no small feat, as more than 1 million people (plus all of their possessions and livestock) are leaving. Plus, Pharaoh's army is in hot pursuit. How does God deliver them from the Egyptian army? (Exodus 13:17-15:21)

8. Put yourself in the Israelites' shoes. In light of God delivering you from the Egyptians, what would you be thinking about Him and what He is like?

9. List the many ways God provides for His people in the desert. How does God continually provide for you? (Exodus 15 – 18)

Week 2: The Law
Scripture: Exodus 19 – 20

1. Where are Moses and the Israelites when God gives them the Law? (Exodus 19)

2. God is using Moses to speak to the people for Him. How does God appear to Moses? What is the purpose of this? (Exodus 19:9)

3. Thunder, lightning, thick clouds, fire, smoke, and trumpet blasts are all used to signal the Lord's presence. What is the purpose of these manifestations? Why is there a death sentence upon any who would touch the mountain? (Exodus 19)

4. God gives Moses the Ten Commandments. Write down the commandments and a brief description of what each one means.

5. The Ten Commandments give a good summary of the Law, although more specifics can be found in the rest of Exodus and Leviticus. In Mark 12:30-31, Jesus

gives two commands. How does obeying these two commands relate to following all of the Law outlined in Exodus and Leviticus?

_____

_____

_____

Week 3: The People Rebel
Scripture: Numbers 11 – 14

1. Dissention begins to disrupt the Israelite camp. What are the people complaining about? How might this foreshadow things to come when they explore the Promised Land? (Numbers 11; 13)

_____

_____

_____

2. How does Moses respond to the complaints of the people? What is God's solution to the complaints of the people?

_____

_____

_____

3. What do the Israelites want? What does God give them? What is the result of their insistence on having their own way? (Chapter 11)

_____

_____

_____

4. What are Aaron and Miriam complaining about? What lesson can you learn about speaking poorly of God's anointed? (Chapter 12)

_____

_____

_____

5. How does Moses react to his siblings' grumbling? How might you have reacted? What would the appropriate reaction be?

6. What is the report from those who explored the Promised Land? Does Caleb agree with the report? How does his report differ? (Chapter 13)

7. How does the community react to the reports? What do they want to do? What are they focused on? (Chapter 14)

8. What is God's response to the reports? What is His reasoning?

9. Moses intercedes on behalf of the people. What arguments does he make? What does this teach you about the importance of prayer?

10. What is God's final judgment on the community? How might you be grumbling against the Lord in any areas of your life? What could you do to change your attitude?

Week 4: 40 Years of Wandering
Scripture: Numbers 20 – 25; Deuteronomy 24 – 31

1. Because they rebelled against God, the Israelites have to wander in the desert until everyone 21 and older dies. Why are Moses and Aaron *also* not permitted to enter the Promised Land? (Numbers 20)

2. The people continue to grumble. What are they crying out for? (Numbers 21:5)

3. Why does this generation need to pass away before the new one can take hold of the Promised Land?

4. The Israelites encounter war as they wander. What is God using these encounters to prepare the people for?

5. Israel is seduced by Moab. Why is it dangerous for Israel to interact with Moab? (Numbers 25) How does God solve this problem?

6. Christians can also be seduced by the world. What temptations do you think are common in the world today? How are you tempted to follow in the ways of the world? What can you do about it?

7. Moses dies and is given an epitaph in Deuteronomy 34. What does God say about Moses? If you died today, what would God say about you?

Monthly Reflection
How did this month's study help you ...

1. Understand the Bible as a continuous story?

2. See God's salvation plan for man?

3. Learn how to study the Bible?

4. Grow in your personal walk with Jesus?

PROMISED LAND

Promised Land

How difficult is it to wait for something you eagerly desire?

Pretty hard! Whether it's something small (like eating dessert after dinner or opening presents on Christmas morning) or something life-changing (like getting married to your spouse or finally meeting a new baby) ... waiting isn't easy.

And patience is especially hard to come by in today's "instant gratification" culture. From fast food to the Internet, so much is at our fingertips that, when something doesn't happen instantaneously — frustration erupts.

But God is infinitely patient. Just look at Israel ...

God has waited for 40 years — for an entire generation of Israelites to pass away — before bringing His people to the Promised Land (also known as Canaan). And it's the land He had promised Abraham several generations before that.

> **God has been patient for *hundreds* of years, but the day has finally arrived. At long last, Israel will get a place to call home!**

God has been patient for *hundreds* of years, but the day has finally arrived. At long last, Israel will get a place to call home!

As Israel claims the Promised Land under the leadership of Joshua — one of only two people to survive the desert wanderings (the other was Caleb) — you'll see God rewarding faith and patience ...

And He does it by showing Himself faithful. With this grand entrance into Canaan, God honors the faith of Joshua and Caleb, who believed the Lord would deliver the land to them ... as well as the faith of Abraham, Isaac, and Jacob, who believed the promise without ever seeing it come to pass.

Scripture Coverage: Joshua
Scripture Reading: Joshua
Book Genre: Historical
Main Theme: God's people subdue the Promised Land by faith
Main Events: Jordan; Jericho; Conquering the Land; Dominion of the Land
Main Characters: Joshua

Week 1: Jordan
Scripture: Joshua 1 – 4

1. Israel is under new leadership. How has God prepared Joshua to lead Israel? (Exodus 17:8-16; Exodus 24:12-18; Numbers 14)

2. God encourages Joshua three times to "be strong and courageous." Why do you think Joshua needs this encouragement? (Joshua 1)

3. What powerful instruction does God tell Joshua to obey? Why is this so important? How can you apply this in your life today? (Joshua 1:7-8)

4. Who is Rahab? What does she do for the Israelite spies? (Joshua 2)

5. What confession of faith does Rahab make to the spies? What can we learn about God's character in sparing "this kind of woman?"

6. What deal do the spies make with Rahab?

7. How does the nation of Israel cross the Jordan River? Other than providing safe passage for His people, why does God perform this miracle?

8. The people set up a memorial to commemorate the passage through the river. Why do they do this? (Joshua 4)

9. These stones remind the Israelites of God's goodness, a symbol of a time when God protected and provided for them. Looking back on your life, write about a time when God moved on your behalf.

Week 2: Jericho
Scripture: Joshua 5 – 6

1. In addition to boosting the Israelites' faith, what impact did the miracle in the Jordan River make? (Joshua 5:1)

2. What happens to the manna? What is the significance of this? (Joshua 5:12)

3. Who does Joshua meet? (Joshua 5:13)

4. What does this meeting teach us about God's presence in our lives during struggles?

5. What obstacles are you facing right now? Write down a prayer of faith affirming your knowledge that God is always with us.

6. God gives specific instructions to Joshua about attacking the city of Jericho. What does this tell you about God's character? How might you go about finding God's instructions when you face difficult circumstances?

7. What happens as a result of the Israelites following God's instructions? (Joshua 6)

8. Why is this first victory over Jericho, a fortified city and an eastern gateway to the land of Canaan, so important to the Israelites?

9. When God gives a command to wipe out all the living in the city, it can seem contradictory to His attributes of love and righteousness. Looking back, how might we understand this command as consistent with God's loving character? (Joshua 6:21; Deuteronomy 12:31; 18:3-9; 20:18; Genesis 6:5-7)

Week 3: Conquering the Land
Scripture: Joshua 7 – 12

1. How does Achan sin? What are the consequences of his actions? What does this teach you about the consequences of your own sin?

2. After Achan's sin is uncovered, what is the result of the Israelite's second attack on Ai? (Joshua 8; Numbers 32:23)

3. What does Joshua read to the crowd? Why do you think he does this? (Joshua 8:34-35)

4. How do the Gibeonites trick Israel? Why? What is Israel's mistake? What lesson can you learn from this error? (Joshua 9)

5. Kings in neighboring lands form an alliance to attack Gibeon. What command does God give Joshua about them? Name three specific ways in which God is fighting for Israel against these kings? (Joshua 10)

6. God continues to give Israel victory, and they conquer the Southern and Northern kingdoms. What is God doing to the hearts of Israel's enemies? Why? How will this help Israel?

7. God has given Israel the land of Canaan as an inheritance, but the people have to fight for the land. Why doesn't God just drive the people out instead of making Israel fight? How does this apply to us and the fighting we must do?

Week 4: Dominion of the Land
Scripture: Joshua 13 – 24

1. The Lord divides the inheritance of the land among the tribes of Israel. What characteristics of God are displayed in the detailed account of who goes where? (Joshua 13 – 22)

2. What do you learn about God from Joshua 21:43-45? How does knowing that God keeps His word encourage you?

3. What encouragement does Joshua give the leaders of Israel? According to Romans 12:8, encouragement is a gift. Why is it so important to encourage others? How do you feel when you are being encouraged? (Joshua 23)

4. What warnings does Joshua give the leaders? How can you apply these warnings to your life today? (Joshua 23)

5. Joshua presents the Israelites with a choice. What choice are they given? What choice have you made? Does your life reflect this choice? (Joshua 24:15)

Monthly Reflection
How did this month's study help you ...

1. Understand the Bible as a continuous story?

2. See God's salvation plan for man?

3. Learn how to study the Bible?

4. Grow in your personal walk with Jesus?

JUDGES

Judges

Bad habits die hard — once begun, they can be nearly impossible to stop.

No one knows this truth better than Israel. After Joshua's death, the people fail to obey God's command to remove the other nations inhabiting the Promised Land. Slowly but surely — over the next 400 years — the Israelites become corrupted by these neighboring groups, falling into idolatry and immorality.

So begins a sinful cycle, which is illustrated seven times within the Book of Judges:
1. Israel falls into sin and idolatry
2. Israel becomes enslaved
3. Israel cries out for deliverance
4. God raises a judge
5. God delivers Israel

> **Judges operate not in a courtroom but on a battlefield, leading Israel's military campaigns to free the enslaved tribes from oppressive nations.**

Though we understand a judge as someone presiding over a dispute in a court of law, the judges God calls up to deliver Israel are different. These judges operate not in the courtroom but on a battlefield, leading Israel's military campaigns to free the enslaved tribes from oppressive nations.

Typically, these judges receive lifetime appointments from God. But once the judge dies, the sin cycle quickly starts up again, so God raises up a new judge to fight for His people.

As the Father proves Himself faithful (once again) in the midst of Israel's pervasive moral and spiritual disobedience, a woman named Ruth (who lived in the same era as the judges) lives a life in stark contrast to her peers. Because of her faithful obedience, God uses her to illustrate the inclusion of Gentiles in His redemption plan, and to foreshadow the future ministry of Jesus.

Scripture Coverage: Judges and Ruth
Scripture Reading: Judges and Ruth
Book Genre: Historical
Main Theme: Judges are chosen to the lead the people over 400 years
Main Events: Deborah; Gideon; Samson; Ruth
Main Characters: Deborah; Gideon; Samson; Ruth

Week 1: Deborah
Scripture: Judges 1 – 5

1. Looking back: What three commands has God given the people? What will happen if they fail to obey? (Deuteronomy 7:1-5)

2. Judges 2:1-23 sets the tone and pattern for the rest of the book. In your own words, describe what is happening and why.

3. What phrase keeps getting repeated? (Judges 3:7,12; 4:1)

4. How long are the Israelites in bondage? Why do you think it takes so long for Israel to cry out for help? What does this tell you about the heart of man? (Judges 4:3)

5. Deborah is introduced. What credentials does she hold? What is her occupation? What does it mean to be a prophetess (or prophet)?[9] (Judges 4:4-5)

6. How does God plan to defeat the army of Jabin? What is Barak's response? What conclusions can you draw from this about Barak's relationship with God?

7. Which aspects of praise and worship do you see in Deborah and Barak's song? How do you celebrate after a great victory? Consider a great victory in your life and write your own song of praise. (Judges 5)

Week 2: Gideon
Scripture: Judges 6 – 8

1. Israel continues to do "evil in the eyes of the Lord." Describe Israel's captivity with the Midianites?

2. Where is Gideon when the angel of the Lord appears to him? How is Gideon addressed?

3. The Lord turns to Gideon, implying that (in this case) the Lord and the angel of the Lord are one in the same. This is referred to as a "Theophany."[10] What does God instruct Gideon to do? What encouragement does He offer? (Judges 6:14-16)

4. According to Matthew 28:20, does God also offer this encouragement to you? How should this hope impact the way you live?

5. What prompts Gideon to act? As believers today, we have that same Spirit within us. What prompts your actions? Does God have full reign in your life? Offer a prayer of surrender for any areas you need to give up to God. (Judges 6:34)

6. Why is the Midianite army so small? Describe Midian's defeat, focusing especially on God's role. (Judges 7)

7. How do the Israelites respond to Gideon and his success in delivering them? God has obviously worked through Gideon, but he still faces criticism for his actions. How does Gideon handle his critics? What does this teach you about criticism? (Judges 8)

8. Consider a time when you have faced opposition. Has someone opposed you, like Gideon, because of your obedience to God? Or, like the Israelites, have you given opposition to God's man? (Judges 8:4-9)

_____

_____

_____

9. Gideon makes a gold ephod,[11] probably with the intention of honoring God. What do the Israelites do with it? How does this action reflect what is in their hearts? What is Gideon's mistake in this situation?

_____

_____

_____

Week 3: Samson
Scripture: Judges 13 – 16

1. God calls Samson to be a Nazirite.[12] What three criteria must be met in order to be a Nazirite? (Numbers 6:1-8)

_____

_____

_____

2. In light of this call, what intentions does God have for Samson?

_____

_____

_____

3. What characteristics does Samson display in Judges 14:1-2?

_____

_____

_____

4. What people are ruling over Israel during this time? Why does God use this Philistine woman to attract Samson?

_____

_____

_____

5. What Nazirite vow does Samson break? Again, what does this tell you about Samson? (Judges 14)

_____

_____

_____

6. What other characteristics do you observe about Samson? (Judges 14)

_____

_____

_____

7. Describe how Samson is used to attack the Philistines.

_____

_____

_____

8. What is Samson's true problem? Where is God on Samson's priority list? (Judges 16:1)

_____

_____

_____

9. What does Samson not realize? Why is this so sad? Why does Samson fail to notice this? (Judges 16:20)

_____

_____

_____

10. What does Samson do — seemingly for the first time — while in captivity? Why do you think it takes hitting rock bottom for man to realize his need for God? Looking

back on your own life, can you relate to Samson in this way?

11. Israel continues to decline morally and spiritually. Consider how far this once godly nation has fallen. Do you notice any similarities between Israel and America today? (Judges 17 – 21)

12. What sums up Israel's problem throughout the Book of Judges? (Judges 21:25)

Week 4: Ruth
Scripture: Ruth

1. Describe the setting of Ruth's story. (Ruth 1)

2. Which law does Ruth take advantage of? (Ruth 2:2; Leviticus 23:22)

3. Consider the phrase, "as it turned out." Who do you see at work in those words? (Ruth 2:3)

4. What is your first impression of Boaz? (Ruth 2:4)

5. What does Boaz generously offer Ruth?

6. In Ruth 2, what hints do you notice connecting the time of Ruth's story to the time of Judges?

7. What is the significance of Ruth lying down at Boaz's feet? What about the guardian-redeemer offering his sandal and Boaz acquiring the land? (Ruth 3 – 4)

8. What testimony is given about Naomi? What does this say about her faith and God's faithfulness? (Ruth 4:14-15)

9. Boaz acquires Ruth as his wife with a dual purpose of providing her the protection of marriage and ensuring that her late husband's name is not blotted out forever. Boaz is often referred to as a "type" of Christ, meaning that God uses the actions of Boaz to foreshadow the coming Messiah. What correlation do you see between Boaz and Jesus? (Ruth 4:10)

10. Ruth's story ends with the genealogy of David. Why is this important?

Monthly Reflection
How did this month's study help you ...

1. Understand the Bible as a continuous story?

2. See God's salvation plan for man?

3. Learn how to study the Bible?

4. Grow in your personal walk with Jesus?

KINGDOM

Kingdom

You've probably read this warning somewhere: "Smoking causes lung cancer, heart disease, emphysema, and may complicate pregnancy."

Thanks to the Surgeon General, the risks of smoking are displayed prominently on all cigarette advertising and packaging. Yet, despite knowing the dangers of smoking, people continue to purchase cigarettes. Millions are sold every day. In the United States alone, half a million people die every year as a result of ignoring the Surgeon General's warnings.

Tragically, Israel isn't very good at heeding caution either.

> ## The Israelites disregard God's warning. They still want a king. So He gives them what they want.

Though God desires to lead His chosen people, they reject Him — wanting instead to have a king in charge. So God, like the Surgeon General, issues warnings about what will happen if they choose this path. *A king will take your sons and compel them to serve in his army. He will take your income and possessions as his own. You will cry out for relief, but it will not come.*

The Israelites disregard God's warning. They still want a king. So He gives them what they want. Just like that, Israel goes from a theocracy[13] — a nation led by God — to a monarchy.

The first king, Saul, doesn't make a very good leader. Eventually, he is replaced by Israel's most famous king, David. Though David rules a united kingdom, Israel fragments in the hands of his descendants. Judah (the southern kingdom) consists of the tribes of Judah and Benjamin, while Israel (the northern kingdom) is made up of the other ten tribes.

Eventually, God's patience with both kingdoms comes to an end. Righteous kings are hard to find in the southern kingdom and non-existent in the northern kingdom. Because of their sinfulness and disobedience, God allows each kingdom to be conquered and taken into captivity by a neighboring nation.

As you'll see throughout Israel's era of monarchial rule, God isn't stingy with opportunities to choose. But neither is He sparing with the consequences of wrong choices.

> **Scripture Coverage:** 1 Samuel – 2 Chronicles
> **Scripture Reading:** 1 Samuel 1 – 18; 2 Samuel; 1 Kings 1 – 15; 2 Kings 17, 25
> **Book Genre:** Historical
> **Main Theme:** Israel becomes a Kingdom, faces judgment for its sin, and is sent into exile
> **Main Events:** Samuel and Saul; David; Solomon; Kingdoms of Israel
> **Main Characters:** Samuel; Saul; David; Solomon

Week 1: Samuel and Saul
Scripture: 1 Samuel 1 - 15

1. Describe the events surrounding Samuel's birth. (1 Samuel 1)

2. Why is Samuel confused about who is calling to him? What does Samuel learn? How can you apply this to hearing God's voice in your own life? (1 Samuel 3)

3. Samuel becomes a judge. In what ways is this account similar to many of the stories from Judges? (1 Samuel 7)

4. Israel asks for a king. Why do the people want a king? What have you wanted that you knew wouldn't be good for you? (1 Samuel 8)

5. Who are the Israelites rejecting when they ask for a king? Think back to the experience you shared in question 4. Was your desire based in ignorance, or were you rejecting God and His ways?

_____

_____

_____

6. Who is anointed the first king of Israel? What type of man is he?

_____

_____

_____

7. How does God establish Saul's kingship? (1 Samuel 11)

_____

_____

_____

8. What great leadership qualities does Samuel display in his farewell speech? (1 Samuel 12:20-25)

_____

_____

_____

9. Why do you think Saul acts out? What is he rebuked for? What are the consequences? (1 Samuel 10:8, 13)

_____

_____

_____

10. God tests Saul by having him wait until the last minute. Have you ever been in a similar situation? What was the result? Why do you think God sometimes waits until the very end?

_____

_____

_____

11. What wise counsel does Samuel give Saul? God compares rebellion to divination.[14] How are they alike? (1 Samuel 15)

_____

_____

_____

Week 2: David
Scripture: 1 Samuel 16 – 18; 2 Samuel

1. Who chooses David to be King? Why David? What providential act moves David into Saul's service? (1 Samuel 16)

_____

_____

_____

2. What great accomplishment does David achieve? What moves David to do this? What are the results? (1 Samuel 17)

_____

_____

_____

3. David succeeds in battle, but what stirs Saul to jealousy? Who is God for and who is God against? What evidence supports your answers? (1 Samuel 18)

_____

_____

_____

4. Saul is clearly trying to kill David, either by his own hand or that of another. But even Saul realizes that God is with David. What does this teach you about God's hand of protection?

_____

_____

_____

5. Time and again, David spares Saul's life. What are David's reasons for doing this? What does this teach you about trying to promote ourselves or manipulate circumstances to get what we want? (1 Samuel 24, 26)

6. Saul takes his own life, and David ascends to the throne. However, seven years pass between the time David is originally called to be king and when he is finally anointed at Hebron. What does this demonstrate about God's timing and patience? (2 Samuel 2)

7. David becomes king over all of Israel and conquers the Jebusites who live in Jerusalem. He takes up residence there. What is behind David's success? (2 Samuel 5:10)

8. How does David sin? When confronted, how does David respond? How does God respond? (2 Samuel 11 – 12)

9. What are the consequences of David's sin? What does that reflect about God's view of sin?

Week 3: Solomon
Scripture: 1 Kings 1 – 11

1. Before David dies, he charges his son Solomon with the crown. What instructions does he leave? How might you apply these words to your own life? (1 Kings 2:2-3)

2. How is Solomon's relationship with the Lord? What conversation do they have? What is the result? (1 Kings 3)

3. Wisdom is not exclusive to Solomon. What can we do according to James 1:5-8?

4. In what ways is Solomon wise? (1 Kings 4:29-34)

5. What construction projects does Solomon take on? (1 Kings 6 – 7)

6. How does God react to the building of the temple? (1 Kings 9:3)

7. What does God say will remain forever? What is the condition? (1 Kings 9)

8. God's promises are often predicated on our obedience and desire to follow after Him. Name one way in which you are following God wholeheartedly. Name an area in which you need God's help to obey. Pray right now for the Lord's help in obedience.

9. What issue does Solomon have? How is this disobedient to the Lord? (1 Kings 11)

10. What is the result of Solomon's marriages? (1 Kings 11)

11. How is it possible for the wisest man in the world to fall away from God? What does this say about the connection (or lack thereof) between having wisdom and having a heart to serve God? Why is it dangerous to think knowledge is enough to build a relationship with God?

Week 4: Kingdoms of Israel
Scripture: 1 Kings 11 – 15; 2 Kings 17; 25

1. Solomon fails to serve God wholeheartedly. What is the judgment for Solomon's sin? (1 Kings 11:29-39)

2. Solomon dies, and his son Rehoboam succeeds him as king. What request do the people make of him? What is his response? (1 Kings 12)

3. How does Rehoboam's response lead to dividing the kingdom, with Jeroboam leading Israel and Rehoboam leading Judah?

4. Why does Jeroboam create two golden calves? What is God's judgment on Jeroboam? (1 Kings 14:7-14)

5. What kind of king is Rehoboam?

6. Notice the trend in the descriptions of the kings of Israel and Judah throughout 1 and 2 Kings. What three specific pieces of information does the Bible share about each king?

7. What happens to Israel? Why does this happen? Where do the people go?
   (2 Kings 17)

   _____

   _____

   _____

8. What is the fate of Judah? What happens to the people? What happens to the
   temple and the palace? (2 Kings 25)

   _____

   _____

   _____

9. What simple message does God communicate to His people (though they fail to
   grasp it)? Why do you think it is so hard for the Israelites to obey?

   _____

   _____

   _____

10. How do people today struggle with this command, too? In your opinion, what
    problem is at the root of unwillingness to follow God wholeheartedly?

    _____

    _____

    _____

Monthly Reflection
How did this month's study help you ...

1. Understand the Bible as a continuous story?

2. See God's salvation plan for man?

3. Learn how to study the Bible?

4. Grow in your personal walk with Jesus?

EXILE AND RETURN

Exile and Return

"For every action, there is an equal and opposite reaction."

Newton's Third Law of Physics is the scientific version of a Biblical principle: You reap what you sow (Galatians 6:7).

Actions have consequences. If you throw a ball to the ground, it will bounce back up with the same force. If you plant a tomato seed, you will harvest tomatoes.

This concept applies to all parts of life — not just physics and farming. If you act friendly, you will make friends. If you slack off at work, you won't be promoted. If you slander others, you can expect them to do the same to you.

Often, the consequences of our actions are immediate — when you throw a ball, it bounces back instantly. But the judgment of God is more like planting the tomato seed — you can't harvest a tomato the next day. It takes time.

> **Just because judgment doesn't come right away doesn't mean the Israelites will get away with sin. Remember: God is patient.**

The Israelites have done "evil in the eyes of the Lord." And this sinfulness goes on without consequences for hundreds of years — 250 years for the northern kingdom, and 400 for the southern kingdom.

After such a long time, the Israelites might think God is just letting their behavior slide. But just because judgment doesn't come right away doesn't mean the Israelites will get away with sin. Remember: God is patient.

When His judgment finally comes — exile and captivity in foreign lands — it's a tough pill to swallow. Yet God is still faithful and loving, never forsaking the people He has chosen.

Prophets like Ezekiel and Daniel are sent to encourage faithfulness. And later, when the time is right, God uses Ezra, Nehemiah, Esther, and others to protect the people, lead them back to the Promised Land, and restore the temple in Jerusalem.

Yes, actions have consequences. God will not be mocked. But He is able to restore penitent[15] hearts.

> **Scripture Coverage:** Ezekiel; Daniel; Ezra; Nehemiah; Esther
> **Scripture Reading:** Ezekiel 1:1-3, 33, 34:1-10, Daniel, Ezra, Nehemiah, Esther
> **Book Genre:** Prophetical and Historical
> **Main Theme:** Israel is exiled[16] for 70 years then led back to rebuild Jerusalem
> **Main Events:** Exile; Return of the Exiled;. The temple rebuilt. Nehemiah Rebuilds the Wall; Esther
> **Main Characters:** Daniel, Ezra, Nehemiah, Esther

Week 1: Exile
Scripture: Ezekiel 1:1-3; 33; 34:1-10; Daniel

1. What do you learn about Ezekiel the man? About his setting? When is this taking place? (Ezekiel 1:1-3)

2. What does God compare Ezekiel to? What is the purpose of this position? (Ezekiel 33)

3. How should you be like Ezekiel concerning people in your life?

4. Who are the shepherds God refers to? Who are the sheep? What are the shepherds guilty of? What will become of the sheep? (Ezekiel 34:1-10)

5. Where does the Book of Daniel take place? When does it take place? (Daniel 1)

    _____

    _____

    _____

6. Who is Daniel, and how does he set himself apart from the other young men? What does God do for Daniel?

    _____

    _____

    _____

7. How does God continue to elevate Daniel? How is God's name glorified before this pagan[17] nation? (Daniel 2)

    _____

    _____

    _____

8. King Nebuchadnezzar has a dream. What is Daniel's interpretation? (Daniel 4)

    _____

    _____

    _____

9. What does Daniel encourage the king to do? Daniel's directive implies it is still possible for Nebuchadnezzar to repent. What does this knowledge mean for you and for those around you? (Daniel 4:27)

    _____

    _____

    _____

10. What thought causes the king to lose his sanity? How does he get it back? What does this teach you about pride and humility?

    _____

    _____

    _____

11. What is Daniel doing in 9:3? What is the content of his prayer?

_____

_____

_____

12. What is Daniel doing in 10:1-13? What do you learn about the spiritual world from this account?

_____

_____

_____

13. What impresses you most about Daniel's life? Which of his characteristics would you like to adopt?

_____

_____

_____

Week 2: Return of the Exiled
Scripture: Ezra

1. What prophetic promise does God make? (Jeremiah 29:10-14)

_____

_____

_____

2. What does Cyrus proclaim? Who orchestrates this act? Who starts heading back to Jerusalem? (Ezra 1)

_____

_____

_____

3. How are the Israelites acting? How is this different from the way people behaved before the exile? (Ezra 3:1-6)

_____

_____

_____

4. What opposition do the Israelites face? Does this mean God isn't with them? Why might you expect this opposition? (Ezra 4)

_____

_____

_____

5. God's favor is on the Israelites, and the temple is completed. What additional evidence is there to suggest that they are pursuing the Lord again? (Ezra 6:14-18)

_____

_____

_____

6. What kind of man is Ezra? How is God's astounding favor on display in the letter Ezra has been given? (Ezra 7)

_____

_____

_____

7. What old sins do the Israelites start to fall back into? What is their response this time around? How is this response different from their responses before the exile? What does this say about the people and their relationship with the Lord?

_____

_____

_____

8. Consider how your life is more different today than it was before you knew God. To what extent might you have fallen back into old sins? If you have, like Ezra, confess them before the Lord and pray about what practical steps you can take to become right with God again.

_____

_____

_____

Week 3: Nehemiah Rebuilds the Wall
Scripture: Nehemiah

1. What condition is the wall of Jerusalem in? What is Nehemiah's response? How do you respond to bad news? (Nehemiah 1)

2. How does Nehemiah respond to King Artaxerxes' question? What does this tell us about Nehemiah's relationship with God? (Nehemiah 2)

3. Nehemiah shares his vision for rebuilding with the people — a project the Bible calls a "good work." What opposition immediately follows this good work? How does Nehemiah counter this? (Nehemiah 2:17-20)

4. Nehemiah faces additional opposition. What is his response this time? How can you apply this to opposition that you face in your life? (Nehemiah 4)

5. What does Israel do in Nehemiah 8:1-3? How long do they listen? What is their attitude as they listen?

6. What does Israel do daily? Why is this important? How often do you read your Bible? How often do you think you should be reading your Bible? (Nehemiah 8:18)

7. Are the Israelites genuine? What evidence is there to support this? What proclamation do they make? (Nehemiah 9:1-6)

8. What has happened to make this nation so different and fervent for the Lord?

9. Sometimes God allows great difficulties as a reminder to focus (or refocus) on Him. Are you facing a trial right now? Maybe God is trying to get your attention. Take some time to pray and evaluate where you are at with the Lord.

Week 4: Esther
Scripture: Esther

1. Although the Book of Esther is placed after Nehemiah in the Bible, the events actually take place 30 years before Nehemiah returns to Jerusalem. The events in this book lay the groundwork for what transpires in Nehemiah. According to Esther 1:2 and Nehemiah 1:1, where do these events take place?

2. What do we learn about Mordecai and Esther? What secret is Esther hiding? Whose favor does she win? (Esther 2)

_____

_____

_____

3. How does Mordecai incur Haman's wrath? Who (from the Book of Daniel) does Haman remind you of? Why does Mordecai not obey the command?

_____

_____

_____

4. What does Haman decide to do?

_____

_____

_____

5. What does Mordecai ask of Esther? What purpose does he see in Esther's position in the kingdom? What does Esther stand to lose? How does she handle the situation?

_____

_____

_____

6. What act of providence do we see in Esther 6:1?

_____

_____

_____

7. Although this book does not mention God at all, God's fingerprints are all over the book. What other acts of providence do you see? When you look at your own life, do you see God's hand upon it? Think of one or two examples and give God praise and glory!

_____

_____

_____

8. What is Haman's fate? What happens to the Jews?

_____

_____

_____

9. How do these events set the stage for Nehemiah and the favor he finds with his king?

_____

_____

_____

Monthly Reflection
How did this month's study help you ...

1. Understand the Bible as a continuous story?

_____

_____

_____

2. See God's salvation plan for man?

_____

_____

_____

3. Learn how to study the Bible?

_____

_____

_____

4. Grow in your personal walk with Jesus?

_____

_____

_____

THE PROPHETS

The Prophets

Will I get that promotion? When will I get married? Which school should I go to? Will I have children? Grandchildren? How long will I live?

What does the future hold?

Where does the world look for answers? Many turn to fortune tellers, palm readers, crystal balls, tea leaves, and horoscopes.

People have always been fascinated by the future, captivated by the supernatural. But trusting in false prophets like psychics and fortune tellers only leads down a path of destruction. And more often than not, their predictions are inaccurate.

When true prophets – those sent by God – make predictions, every single prophecy is accurate. One false forecast, and you do not have a true prophet.

However, while telling the future is a big part of a true prophet's ministry, that's not *all* prophets do.

> **When true prophets — those sent by God — make predictions, every single prophecy is accurate.**

In the Bible, the bulk of a prophet's ministry is to simply proclaim the teachings of God. Usually, this involved:

1) Exposing sin and calling people to a higher moral standard.
2) Warning the Israelites of a coming judgment if they fail to repent.
3) Proclaiming the coming Messiah.

This often overlooked role of a prophet may explain why 12 of the 17 prophetical books in the Bible take place during the time of 2 Kings — as the nation of Israel desperately needs to be called to repentance. These books of prophecy also predict the consequences (including the Exile) if Israel doesn't listen.

Each of the remaining prophetic books also minister during times of great need in Israel. Ezekiel and Daniel prophesy during the Exile. Haggai, Zechariah, and Malachi proclaim God's truth during Israel's return to the Promised Land.

> **Scripture Coverage:** Isaiah – Malachi (for Ezekiel and Daniel, see "Exile and Return" on page 49)
> **Scripture Reading:** Various verses throughout the Prophetical books
> **Book Genre:** Prophetical
> **Main Theme:** God uses the prophets to proclaim His Word for both the future and the present
> **Main Events:** See the general descriptions of each book
> **Main Characters:** Prophets

Week 1: Isaiah, Jeremiah, Lamentations
Scripture: Verses throughout Isaiah, Jeremiah, Lamentations

Isaiah: Confronts Israel with their sins and their coming judgment, speaks against other nations, prophesies about future Jewish exiles and the Messiah.

1. How does Isaiah see himself? How does God help his condition? What does this encounter look like to you? (Isaiah 6)

2. What question does God ask? What is Isaiah's response? What would your response be? Are you truly willing to go wherever God leads you? Be truthful to yourself.

3. What is Isaiah prophesying about in 9:1-7? Share one part of this prophecy that really strikes you.

4. What Old Testament and New Testament prophecies do we see in Isaiah 40:1-5?
(Hint: Verses 1-2 have to do with Judah, and verses 3-5 are about a man who comes just before Christ.)

5. Why do you think God foretells future events in Scripture?

Jeremiah: Prophesies about inevitable judgment when Israel rebels against God and restoration.

1. When does Jeremiah's ministry take place?

2. What do you learn about God's plan for Jeremiah? His plan for you? (Jeremiah 1:5)

3. What is Jeremiah talking about in 3:6-10? What analogy does God use? What sad statement do we see concerning Judah?

4. What does the Lord mean by "New Covenant"? How does this involve Jesus? (Jeremiah 31:31-34)

Lamentations: Five laments that express great sorrow and pain over the destruction of Jerusalem.

1. Describe the scene that is set in Lamentations 1.

   _____

   _____

   _____

2. Who is to blame for the fall of this city?

   _____

   _____

   _____

3. What hope is brought forth in Lamentations 3:21-33? What attributes of God do you see in these verses?

   _____

   _____

   _____

4. As born-again Christians, we are not immune to sin. How can we apply the hope found in Lamentations 3 when we fall into sin?

   _____

   _____

   _____

Week 2: Joel, Micah, Habakkuk, Zephaniah
Scripture: Verses throughout Joel, Micah, Habakkuk, Zephaniah

Joel: Starts with the devastation caused by a plague of locusts,[19] then calls Israel to repentance with a warning of further danger approaching, and reveals prophecy about Israel's future restoration.

1. In Joel, God frequently refers to the "day of the Lord." Locate 2 or 3 instances of this within the book. Based on context, what do you think this phrase means?

   _____

   _____

2. The prophecy in Joel 2:28-32 begins to be fulfilled in Acts 2. In fact, Peter quotes this passage. What does this prophecy mean for believers today?

_____

_____

_____

Micah: Warns Israel of divine judgment and foretells the coming of the Messiah.[20]

1. Micah 5:1-5 refers to the coming Messiah. Where do you see that reference in these verses? What attributes of Christ are foretold?

_____

_____

_____

2. What case is the Lord making in Micah 6:3-5? Is this a case God could make with us today? With you?

_____

_____

_____

Habakkuk: Describes living by faith and shares prophecy about how God will deal with all wickedness in due time.

1. What complaints does Habakkuk voice in chapter 1? Have you ever had similar feelings?

_____

_____

_____

2. What answer does God give in Habakkuk 2:4? Is this reply sufficient for you?

_____

_____

_____

3. Habakkuk's prayer in chapter 3 is a response to God. What does the prayer reveal about Habakkuk? Is trusting God, even when things aren't going the way you wish, something you struggle with? If so, take some time to pray for greater faith.

_____

_____

_____

Zephaniah: Warns the Jews about the coming judgment of God on Judah and the whole Earth.

1. What destruction is coming? Who is it against? Has it happened yet? (Zephaniah 1:2-3)

_____

_____

_____

2. According to Zephaniah 1:14, when will this come to pass? What other book of the Bible does this remind you of? What comfort, as a Christian, can you have concerning these prophecies?

_____

_____

_____

Week 3: Hosea, Amos, Jonah, Nahum, Obadiah

Scripture: Verses throughout Hosea, Amos, Jonah, Nahum, Obadiah

Hosea: Reveals prophecy to Israel about the last call to repentance, how God maintains His love despite Israel's rebellion, and the coming consequences for disobedience.

1. Hosea's relationship with his wife paints a picture of God's relationship with Israel. What happens between Hosea and Gomer? Who does Hosea represent? Gomer? (Hosea 1 – 3)

2. What does God promise in Hosea 14? What does this say about God's longsuffering for us?

Amos: Calls for Israel to repent and for judgment to come down on surrounding nations.

1. What are the Israelites guilty of? Are they an affluent people? What does this say about materialism and God's blessings? In your own experience, does success draw you closer to God or pull you further away? (Amos 6:1-7)

Jonah: Writes this prophetical book as a historical narrative and calls Assyria's capital city, Nineveh, to repentance.

1. What characteristics do you see in Jonah? Have you ever run away from God? What is the result for Jonah? For you? (Jonah 1:3)

2. What somewhat-surprising response do the people of Nineveh have to Jonah's judgment? What is God's reaction?

3. How does Jonah feel about Assyria's repentance? Have you ever been angry with the Lord? How do you deal with that anger?

    _____

    _____

    _____

Nahum: Writes more than 130 years after Jonah and shares prophecy with Assyria about the judgment and destruction that will come upon them, especially on Nineveh.

1. What attribute of God do you see in Nahum 1:2. Why might this lead to judgment?

    _____

    _____

2. What are some of the reasons Nineveh is being judged? What have we learned about God when it comes to sin and judgment? (Nahum 3:1-4)

    _____

    _____

    _____

Obadiah: Reveals prophecy about judgment on Edom for rejoicing over Judah's suffering.

1. Who is the Patriarch of Edom? (Obadiah 1:10; Genesis 27)

    _____

    _____

    _____

2. What is Edom guilty of? In light of this, how should you treat your neighbors? (Obadiah 1:11-14)

    _____

    _____

    _____

Week 4: Haggai, Zechariah, Malachi
Scripture: Verses throughout Haggai, Zechariah, Malachi

<u>Haggai</u>: Exhorts the rebuilding of the temple and calls Israel to holiness.

1. What does God call Zerubbabel and Joshua to do?

2. In Haggai, the Lord often says "give careful thought." What should we give careful thought to? What might this look like for you?

<u>Zechariah</u>: Offers encouragement to rebuilding of the temple for those who are disheartened that the Messiah has not appeared immediately, plus shares eight visions that show God's love and Israel's future destiny.

1. What is the opening plea in chapter 1?

2. What Messianic prophecy does Zechariah 9:9 refer to? Write the Scripture verse below to back this up. Do the same for Zechariah 13:7.

<u>Malachi</u>: Calls Israel to repent of sin, remove those things which hinder their walk with God, and to return fully to God with obedient hearts.

1. God says "Esau I have hated" in Malachi 1:3. Knowing that God loves man, what do you think this means in its context?

    _____

    _____

    _____

2. Malachi presents God's Word in a question-and-answer format. Choose any one question that God asks, and then share your thoughts about how it is answered.

    _____

    _____

    _____

3. What promised blessings come from giving the tithe?[21] (Malachi 3:10)

    _____

    _____

    _____

4. Giving financially is commanded by God to support His work and demonstrate submission and obedience to His authority. Do you tithe? If not, why not? Do you have a Biblical reason for your answer?

    _____

    _____

    _____

Monthly Reflection
How did this month's study help you ...

1. Understand the Bible as a continuous story?

   _____

   _____

   _____

2. See God's salvation plan for man?

   _____

   _____

   _____

3. Learn how to study the Bible?

   _____

   _____

   _____

4. Grow in your personal walk with Jesus?

   _____

   _____

   _____

POETICAL

Poetical

Remember Shakespeare in high school English class?

Soon after you open the Psalms or Proverbs, you'll notice that Biblical books of poetry differ stylistically from the plays and sonnets of Mr. Shakespeare in two key ways:

1) David and Solomon's poetry doesn't rhyme. You won't find couplets, quatrains, or any other rhyme schemes in these poetic books.
2) In Biblical poetry, rhythmic meter cannot be found. When you read Ecclesiastes aloud, you won't hear iambic pentameter or notice any particular beat or cadence to the words.

You may wonder, "Without rhyme and rhythm, how can you classify these books as poetry?"

> **Through these more artistic writing styles, God is able to explore the themes presented in each of the books in unique, meaningful ways.**

The answer: it's because either 1) they were written with the intention of being accompanied by music (like the Psalms), or 2) they utilize literary techniques like simile, metaphor, personification, parallelism,[22] and figure of speech[23] (like Proverbs).

Through these more artistic writing styles, God is able to explore the themes presented in each of the books in unique and meaningful ways.

Job (sometimes described as an opera) explores the connection between God's sovereignty and man's suffering through a series of debates with friends.

Psalms, from King David and several other authors, offer up beautiful prayers and songs, typically falling into the categories of praise, thanksgiving, or lament.[24]

In the Book of Proverbs,[25] Solomon imparts wisdom and offers answers to tough questions using an instruction poetry style made up of short adages.

Solomon also considers the futility of earthly pursuits in Ecclesiastes and creates a godly picture of romance, love, and marriage in Song of Solomon (sometimes called Song of Songs).

> **Scripture Coverage:** Job – Song of Songs
> **Scripture Reading:** Various verses throughout the Poetical books, including all of Ecclesiastes and Song of Songs
> **Book Genre:** Poetical
> **Main Theme:** God's message is communicated poetically through a number of different literary techniques
> **Main Events:** Job; Psalms; Proverbs; Ecclesiastes and Song of Songs
> **Main Characters:** Job; David; Solomon

Week 1: Job
Scripture: Verses throughout Job

1. What kind of man is Job? (Job 1:1-2:10)

2. From the same verses, what do we learn about God, Satan, and the nature of their relationship?

3. What do you learn about God's protection over you? What comfort does that provide you?

4. What trouble befalls Job? What is Job's response?

5. Think about the most recent difficulty you have faced. What was your response in that situation? Why do you think you encountered this difficulty? Who is in charge of your life? What should your attitude be when facing trials?

_____

_____

_____

6. Summarize God's words to Job in chapters 38 – 41.

_____

_____

_____

7. How does Job respond to God? (Job 42:1-6)

_____

_____

_____

8. What is the final outcome for Job after this trial? (Job 42)

_____

_____

_____

9. Considering Job's story, how should you look upon the circumstances in your life? How do you see God when it comes to day-to-day living? Is God truly the Lord of your life?

_____

_____

_____

Week 2: Psalms
Scripture: Various Psalms

1. Read Psalms 8, 30, 32. Categorize each one as a Psalm of either Thanksgiving, Praise, or Lament. Support each answer with a verse.

2. Some Psalms are Messianic[26] or have Messianic verses within them. Find the verses that relate to the coming of Jesus in Psalms 2, 16, and 68.

3. Many Psalms are written as prayers. Find a Psalm, perhaps you already have a favorite, and recite it to God as a prayer.

Week 3: Proverbs
Scripture: Various Proverbs

1. Who is the main author of Proverbs?

2. What is the purpose of Proverbs? (Proverbs 1:1-7)

3. In Proverbs 10, you'll start to see some of the literary techniques mentioned in the "Poetical" introduction (i.e. simile, metaphor, personification, etc). List two or three of the techniques you find and the verses they go with.

4. Choose any chapter from Proverbs 10 – 29. Read it and share one or two particular proverbs that speak to you. How can you apply them to your life?

Week 4: Ecclesiastes and Song of Songs
Scripture: Ecclesiastes and Song of Songs

1. Solomon is generally considered the author of Ecclesiastes. Look at Chapter 1:1,16 and 12:9. What clues do these verses offer which would suggest that Solomon is the author?

2. What point is Solomon making in Ecclesiastes 1:1-11? Have you ever felt this way?

3. Solomon repeats two expressions throughout this book: "Under the sun" and "Chasing after the wind." What do you think he means by these two expressions?

4. Make a list of the things Solomon finds meaningless throughout Ecclesiastes. Support this list with Scripture.

5. What do you think God means by "setting eternity in the hearts of men?" (Ecclesiastes 3:11)

6. What piece of advice is offered in Ecclesiastes 5:1-3? To what extent do you view God with reverence? To what extent might you be taking your relationship with God for granted?

7. What common destiny befalls every person? Knowing this, might it be prudent to think of eternity and how to approach it? (Ecclesiastes 9)

8. Where can meaning be found? (Ecclesiastes 12)

9. It's easy to forget that "God will bring every deed into judgment, including every hidden thing." Do you live your life in light of this truth? (Ecclesiastes 12:14)

10. What does Song of Songs repeatedly warn against? (Song of Songs 2:7; 3:5; 8:4)

_____

_____

_____

11. Virginity until marriage is God's standard. As Song of Songs shows, sex is a gift from God — to be enjoyed within the context of a marriage between a man and a woman. How does this directive differ from the world's view of sex? Does it differ from your view of sex? What steps can you take to honor God in this area? (Song of Songs 4:12; Genesis 2:24; Hebrews 13:4)

_____

_____

_____

Monthly Reflection
How did this month's study help you ...

1. Understand the Bible as a continuous story?

_____

_____

_____

2. See God's salvation plan for man?

_____

_____

_____

3. Learn how to study the Bible?

_____

_____

_____

4. Grow in your personal walk with Jesus?

_____

_____

_____

CHRIST ON EARTH

Christic on Earth

Think of your favorite book or movie.

What problem or conflict lies before the main character in the story?

More than likely this conflict involves an enemy — another person, a force of nature, a society or culture — standing in the hero's way.

Toward the end of the story, you may also remember a tense, exciting scene in which everything the story has been building toward comes to a head. Perhaps there is even a throw-down battle between a hero and a villain. Two forces enter, but only one leaves. This is the climax — and by the time it's over, the conflict will be resolved.

If you think of the Bible as one long story, then the life, death, and resurrection of Jesus Christ all make up the climax. Jesus arrives and defeats his enemies — death and Satan — in one fell swoop.

> **Everything God has been building toward throughout the Old Testament culminates at this point.**

Everything God has been building toward throughout the Old Testament culminates at this point. The Messiah — prophesied about since Genesis, foreshadowed through Isaac, Boaz, and other Christ "types" — has finally arrived to deliver His people. And by the time the Gospels conclude, the conflict is resolved — Christ[27] leaves the tomb victorious!

This is the most thrilling story in all of Scripture — the one the salvation of the world rests upon. And it's recounted in four different books: the Gospels,[28] written by Matthew, Mark, Luke, and John.

While each of these accounts share the story of Christ, they also emphasize a different aspect of His life on Earth. Matthew focuses on fulfillment of prophecy and Israel's hope. Mark shows Him to be the Son of God. Luke concentrates on the teachings of Christ. And John emphasizes Jesus' divine nature as God incarnate.[29]

From birth to resurrection,[30] no matter which Gospel account you read, it doesn't get better than this ... God's pièce de résistance.

> **Scripture Coverage:** Matthew – John
> **Scripture Reading:** One of the Four Gospels
> **Book Genre:** Historical
> **Main Theme:** Jesus comes and offers salvation through His death and resurrection
> **Main Events:** Pre-Ministry; Public Ministry; Ministry to the Disciples; Death and Resurrection
> **Main Characters:** Jesus; The Disciples[31]

Week 1: Pre-Ministry
Scripture: Verses throughout the Gospels

1. Describe the charge Mary is given by the angel Gabriel. What is Mary's response? Would you react the same way? (Luke 1 – 2)

2. Matthew 1 relates the account of Mary's pregnancy and Jesus' birth from Joseph's perspective. What kind of man does the Bible say he is?

3. How has the world changed from the Israelite nation? Compare the rulers in days of Nehemiah and Ezra to those in power during the time when Jesus was born. Where do Joseph and Mary reside? Where do they go? Why do they go? (Luke 2)

4. Where is Jesus born? How does His birthplace signify the kind of life Jesus would live?

    _____

    _____

    _____

5. Why do Joseph and Mary flee to Egypt? When do they return? And where do they go after Egypt? (Matthew 2)

    _____

    _____

    _____

6. The only Biblical accounts of Jesus as a boy are found in Luke 2. What happens when Jesus is 12 years old? What is He doing? What does the Bible say about His growth?

    _____

    _____

    _____

7. What does John mean by calling Jesus "the Word" in 1:1-18? What divine[32] aspect of Jesus is referred to by saying "He was with God in the beginning"? What else do we learn about Jesus from these verses?

    _____

    _____

    _____

Week 2: Public Ministry
Scripture: John 2 – 12

1. John 2 records Christ's first public miracle. What is it? Besides the immediate need, what is His purpose in performing that miracle?

    _____

    _____

    _____

2. Jesus discusses being born again with Nicodemus. What does it mean to be "born again?" Are you? How do you know? (John 3)

_____

_____

_____

3. What miraculous sign does Jesus give the Samaritan woman? What declaration does Jesus make at the end of their discussion? (John 4)

_____

_____

_____

4. Jesus breaks cultural boundaries by associating with the Samaritan woman. Are there any boundaries you face today? How might you break through them?

_____

_____

_____

5. Many Samaritans believed in God because of the woman's testimony. Think about your testimony and how you might share it. (John 4)

_____

_____

_____

6. Jesus feeds the multitude. What does He use to feed so many? What can you offer to Jesus to use and multiply? (John 6)

_____

_____

_____

7. Christ heals a blind man. Why had he been born blind, according to people in the community? What explanation does Jesus offer? How can you surrender the troubling areas of your life to God, so that, in His sovereignty,[33] He can use them to be glorified in your life? (John 9)

_____

_____

_____

8. Jesus faces conflict with some of the Jews, escalating to the point that they attempt to stone Him. What problem do they have with Jesus? How does He respond? (John 8 – 10)

9. Why is Lazarus sick? After Lazarus dies, why does Jesus weep? What does that say about His thoughts towards you and your trials? (John 11)

10. How does Christ raising Lazarus from the dead show the power of God? How is this comforting to us who believe?

11. What does Jesus say about His coming death? What does God the Father say about it? (John 12)

Week 3: Ministry to the Disciples
Scripture: John 13-17

1. Why does Jesus wash the disciples' feet? (John 13)

2. What does Jesus command his disciples to do in John 13:34? What purpose does this command have? As a follower of Christ, do you keep that command? Is there a brother or sister in the Lord you might have to work on loving more? What practical step can you take to improve this relationship?

---

3. What does Jesus promise to do? How does anyone come to know God? According to Jesus, is there any other way to God? What implications does this have for you, for your family, for the world? (John 14:1-7)

---

4. How can you know if someone loves Jesus? Look at your life in view of God's commands. If someone looks at your life, will they be able to tell that you love Jesus by the way you live? (John 14:15)

---

5. How does John 15:18-25 explain the treatment of Christians in the world today?

---

6. Why is it important that Jesus goes away? What will the Holy Spirit do? (John 16:5-16)

---

7. What two reasons does God have for loving us? What do you think "love" means? (John 16:27)

---

8. How does Jesus pray for Himself? Wouldn't it be awesome if we could legitimately pray John 17:4?

_____

_____

_____

9. How does Jesus pray for His disciples?

_____

_____

_____

10. What does Jesus pray for all believers?

_____

_____

_____

11. After reading these prayers, what is one lesson you can apply to your own prayer life?

_____

_____

_____

Week 4: Death and Resurrection
Scripture: Various Scriptures from the Gospels

1. What does Jesus mean in John 18:21?

_____

_____

_____

2. What does Jesus ask of God? How remarkable is it that a Man who is dying prays for those who are unjustly carrying out His death? How can you take this example and apply it when you have been wronged? (Luke 23:34)

_____

_____

_____

3. Jesus ministers to the thief being crucified next to Him. What does the thief ask? How does this show his faith in Christ as God? What does Jesus promise him?

---

4. Jesus announces "it is finished." What is the "it?" (John 19:30)

---

5. What does Mary Magdalene discover in John 20? What does she find out later?

---

6. Why is the writing of the Gospel of John recorded in Scripture? (John 20:30-31)

---

7. The disciples don't recognize Jesus. Why might this be? What causes John, "the disciple whom Jesus loved," to realize it is Jesus? (John 21)

---

8. Describe the interaction between Jesus and Peter. Why is this important for Jesus to do?

---

9. What is John's testimony concerning Jesus? (John 21:25)

---

10. What is the last command of Jesus? Think hard — are you fulfilling this command? Or have the cares of this world gotten in the way of this goal? (Acts 1:1-8)

_____

_____

_____

Monthly Reflection
How did this month's study help you ...

1. Understand the Bible as a continuous story?

_____

_____

_____

2. See God's salvation plan for man?

_____

_____

_____

3. Learn how to study the Bible?

_____

_____

_____

4. Grow in your personal walk with Jesus?

_____

_____

_____

CHURCH AND GROWTH

Church and Growth

The Great Wall of China and the Body of Christ have a lot in common.

Considered one of the New Seven Wonders of the World, the Great Wall of China is a structure 2,000 years in the making. And because of its size (5,500 miles long — visible from space!) and the amount of work it took to make, the Great Wall is considered a manmade marvel.

Various rulers spanning many generations had citizens and slaves alike constructing this massive wall. Over the years, repairs and additions have been made. Today, the structure is comprised of an estimated 4 billion bricks.

The Body of Christ is a 2,000-year-old project, too — beginning just after Jesus returned to the Father. And like the Great Wall construction, God has used multitudes of people throughout many generations and from a variety of classes — Jews and Gentiles, slaves and free — to help create His Church (Galatians 3:28).

> ## In the Body of Christ, the builders aren't just the bricklayers — they're also the bricks! God's Church is made up of *people.*

But in the Body of Christ, the builders aren't just the bricklayers — they're also the bricks! God's Church is made up of *people.*

The Book of Acts chronicles the very beginning of this building project, and its rapid growth. In the Gospels, Jesus' disciples have already been instructed and trained. Now, they receive the Holy Spirit (as promised) and follow through on Jesus' command to go and spread the Good News.

So the Church begins to grow, penetrating most of the known world — in spite of persecution.

Acts also offers a model for the Body of Christ today. How believers fulfill God's call to be a witness, as well as how they should treat one another, is demonstrated beautifully. As you study, consider how you can follow in the example of the early Church.

> **Scripture Coverage:** Acts
> **Scripture Reading:** Acts
> **Book Genre:** Historical
> **Main Theme:** God establishes and expands the Church through the obedience of His followers
> **Main Events:** Birth of the Church; Church Growth and Persecution; Paul's Missionary Journeys, Paul's Imprisonment
> **Main Characters:** Peter; Paul

Week 1: Birth of the Church
Scripture: Acts 1 – 5

1. About how many believers are there at this time? (Acts 1:15)

2. Where are all the believers on the day of Pentecost?[34] What happens to them?

3. How does the crowd outside perceive what takes place?

4. Consider what Peter is like in the Gospels. How is Peter different in Acts 2? Why do you think he has changed?

5. According to Peter, the promise of the baptism of the Holy Spirit is for whom? (Acts 2:38-39) Do you believe the baptism of the Holy Spirit is for people today? Are you filled with the Holy Spirit? (Acts 2:38-39; Luke 11:13)

6. How many new believers are added that day after Peter's preaching?

7. What do the believers devote themselves to doing? Do you devote yourself to these things? What area(s) might you improve on? (Acts 2:42)

8. Why are Peter and John put in jail? What does the Word say immediately after their imprisonment? (Acts 4)

9. How does the Bible describe Peter when he is asked to give an account?

10. What do the rulers notice about these men? (Acts 4:13)

11. How do Peter and John respond to being ordered to stop proclaiming the name of Jesus? How do you respond when sharing the name of Jesus is not comfortable?

_____

_____

_____

12. How do Ananias and Sapphira sin? Why do you think their punishment is death?

_____

_____

_____

13. What miraculous signs do the apostles perform?

_____

_____

_____

14. Persecution starts to come on the apostles, and they are jailed and beaten for their faith. What is the apostles' response to the flogging they receive? What do they do afterwards?

_____

_____

_____

15. What kind of persecution do you (and other believers) face today? How do you react? Can you testify, like the apostles, that you will never stop proclaiming Christ?

_____

_____

_____

Week 2: Church Growth and Persecution
Scripture: Acts 6 – 12

1. What continues in Acts 6:7?

_____

_____

_____

2. Describe Stephen. Why is he seized? (Acts 6:8)

_____

_____

_____

3. Why is Stephen stoned? Who approved this? (Acts 6:8-8:1)

_____

_____

_____

4. What event immediately follows Stephen's death? Who seems to be the leader behind this? Where do the people go to escape persecution? What do the people continue to do after they are scattered?

_____

_____

_____

5. What does Saul intend to do in Acts 9? What happens to him as he nears Damascus? Think back to your own conversion experience. How has your life changed?

_____

_____

_____

6. Why are the believers who came with Peter astonished? (Acts 10)

_____

_____

_____

7. What does Peter have them do after they receive the Holy Spirit? Water baptism is a public declaration of faith in Jesus. Have you been water baptized? If not, consider taking that step of obedience.

_____

_____

_____

8. Why is Peter criticized by his fellow believers? What does Peter say that quiets the objections? What is their conclusion?

_____

_____

_____

9. How does God use the death of Stephen to further the Gospel? How does this compare to Romans 8:28? Think of a difficult trial you face right now and pray this verse over your life. (Acts 11:19-21)

_____

_____

_____

10. What happens to James? What happens to Peter? How does Peter escape?

_____

_____

_____

11. Why did Herod die?

_____

_____

_____

12. What is still happening in Acts 12:25?

_____

_____

_____

Week 3: Paul's Missionary Journeys
Scripture: Acts 13 – 20

1. Who sends Paul and Barnabas? (Acts 13:4)

_____

_____

_____

2. Who shows up to hear God's Word? How do some of the Jews react? According to verse 46 why do they now preach to the Gentiles?[35] (Acts 13:44-46)

_____

_____

_____

3. What do Paul and Barnabas do regularly? What confirms that their message is the truth? (Acts 14)

_____

_____

_____

4. What happens to Paul in 14:19? What does Paul say in verse 22? Do you find his statement true in your own life? Does it bring perspective?

_____

_____

_____

5. What common church practice is exemplified by Paul and Barnabas in Acts 14:23? Who might you consider an elder today?

_____

_____

_____

6. What issue do the believers in Jerusalem have to deal with? What tools for reconciliation are displayed here that can help you resolve a dispute in your life? (Acts 15)

_____

_____

_____

7. Why are Paul and Silas imprisoned and beaten? What are their attitudes like in prison? Why are they able to praise the Lord?

_____

_____

_____

8. What is the reaction from the Jews in Thessalonica? How is this consistent with people receiving the Gospel today?

_____

_____

_____

9. What are the Bereans commended for? Why is their technique of examining the Scripture against what is preached a good example to follow?

_____

_____

_____

10. What does God command all people to do? What does this imply about all people? What are the consequences for not repenting?

_____

_____

_____

11. What are the highlights of Paul's trip to Ephesus?

_____

_____

_____

Week 4: Paul's Imprisonment
Scripture: Acts 21 – 28

1. When Paul returns to Jerusalem and meets with the brothers, what does he do? Why is it good to share testimonies?

_____

_____

_____

2. Paul's fame catches up with him in Jerusalem. Why is he arrested this time?

_____

_____

_____

3. What do the Jews intend to do to Paul even though he is under Roman guard? (Acts 23)

    _____

    _____

    _____

4. Paul appears before which three governing heads? Why do you think God might allow Paul to appear before all three without being set free? (Acts 24-26)

    _____

    _____

    _____

5. Paul is a Roman citizen and exercises his right to take his case before Caesar, thus they set sail for Rome. What happens on his journey there? (Acts 25:12; 27)

    _____

    _____

    _____

6. Where do Paul and the rest of the crew get shipwrecked?

    _____

    _____

    _____

7. What opportunity does Paul take advantage of to spread the Gospel?

    _____

    _____

    _____

8. Paul is always intentionally looking for opportunities to share Christ. Do you have that mindset? How different would your day-to-day life be if you shared like Paul? Start today, pray and look for chances to share God with the people you run into.

    _____

    _____

    _____

9. What benefits of imprisonment does Paul receive when he gets to Rome?

10. What does Paul continue to do even though he is under house arrest?

11. How long is Paul in Rome?

12. This whole process, from the time he gets arrested in Jerusalem to where he waits in Rome, takes years. Is there a difficult situation you've been facing for a number of years? What hope can you take from what happened to Paul? Pray about this and give it to God.

Monthly Reflection
How did this month's study help you ...

1. Understand the Bible as a continuous story?

2. See God's salvation plan for man?

3. Learn how to study the Bible?

_____

_____

_____

4. Grow in your personal walk with Jesus?

_____

_____

_____

PAULINE EPISTLES

Pauline Epistles

When you flip through your mail, what do you keep your eyes peeled for?

Bills? Flyers? Circulars? Advertisements? No, you get those all the time.

You're looking for letters from loved ones — a rare jewel in your mailbox, especially in today's age of texting, email, and Facebook.

When you get a letter, it means someone actually took the time to sit down and compose a handwritten note ... just for you.

> **King over the entire universe, Creator of Heaven and Earth — took the time to write these letters through Paul.**

And when you come across that colored envelope or handwritten address, you get excited. You pull that letter out and read it before you even finish sorting through the rest of your mail.

Why? It's personal ... special ... rare. Rather than using an electronic device for a quick connection, someone bought a stamp and invested time in you!

Personal letters were probably very meaningful and special in Paul's day, too. Imagine how the believers in Corinth, Ephesus, Thessalonica, and other cities felt when they received a letter from Paul. "He's a busy man, traveling and sharing the Good News all over the world ... and he sat down with a scribe to write to *us*?"

How much more so for the individuals he wrote to, like Timothy, Titus, and Philemon. "Paul wanted to say something to *me* so much that he wrote a letter?"

Taking it one step further, God — King over the entire universe, Creator of Heaven and Earth — took the time to write these letters through Paul. And not just for the early Church.

God sent *you* Paul's letters through the Bible — the 13 Pauline Epistles.

In these letters, God uses Paul to present doctrinal truths and practical applications for resolving specific issues and problems impacting these early believers... issues still relevant for believers today. How appropriate that God would use such an encouraging form of communication to inspire, teach, and guide you in your faith.

> **Scripture Coverage:** Romans – Philemon
> **Scripture Reading:** Romans – Philemon
> **Book Genre:** Epistles
> **Main Theme:** Paul's letters to encourage and instruct in the Christian faith
> **Main Events:** See the general description of each book
> **Main Characters:** Paul, as the only author

Note: Unlike January through October, November and December will focus on reading the text rather than answering questions about the text. This is because the content is so rich and deep! Plus, as a believer under the New Covenant, reading the Epistles will be especially important for your spiritual development — because they provide direct instruction for proper Christian living.

Before you read each Epistle, ask God to speak to you through His Word. As you read, consider how each book lines up with its summary below.

Week 1: Romans and Corinthians
Scripture: Romans; 1 Corinthians; 2 Corinthians

Romans: Provides a complete explanation of the Gospel, and corrects the attitudes between Jews and Gentiles.

1 Corinthians: Corrects serious problems that were reported in the Church, and answers a variety of questions that have been brought to Paul's attention.

2 Corinthians: Encourages the Church, and reprimands those who are acting defiantly.

Week 2: Galatians, Ephesians, and Philippians
Scripture: Galatians; Ephesians; Philippians

Galatians: Deals with the matter of legalism.[37]

Ephesians: Encourages strengthening the Ephesians' relationship with Christ living a life worthy of Him.

Philippians: Encourages joy in the face of trials.

Week 3: Colossians and Thessalonians
Scripture: Colossians; 1 Thessalonians; 2 Thessalonians

Colossians: Discusses the supremacy of Christ.

1 Thessalonians: Encourages perseverance and godly living, and clarifies about believers who die in Christ.

2 Thessalonians: Encourages perseverance and corrects end-time beliefs.

Week 4: Timothy, Titus, and Philemon
Scripture: 1 Timothy; 2 Timothy; Titus; Philemon

1 Timothy: Encourages Timothy to protect the Gospel from false teaching, and offers instructions on church matters.

2 Timothy: Encourages Timothy to preach the Gospel and endure hardships.

Titus: Explains the qualifications for church leadership.

Philemon: Asks Philemon to deal kindly with his runaway slave, Onesimus, and receive him back as a fellow believer.

1. Pick one book you've read this month and write a reflection about how God's Word has spoken to you.

2. How will you change as a result of reading Paul's letters?

_____

_____

_____

_____

_____

Monthly Reflection
How did this month's study help you ...

1. Understand the Bible as a continuous story?

_____

_____

_____

2. See God's salvation plan for man?

_____

_____

_____

3. Learn how to study the Bible?

_____

_____

_____

4. Grow in your personal walk with Jesus?

_____

_____

_____

G E N E R A L E P I S T L E S

General Epistles

An unforgettable moment in Olympic history ...

Derek Redmond, a British runner in the 1992 Summer Games, starts running in the semi-finals of the 400-meter dash. As he rounds a bend in the track, a powerful pain suddenly shoots up the back of his leg.

Derek slows and eventually falls to the ground. He has torn his hamstring.

Medical staff members run to Derek's side, but he waves them off. Standing to his feet, Derek begins limping toward the finish line. As Derek approaches the final stretch of the race, his father runs to meet him on the field. With his father supporting him, they finish the race together.

Most people have forgotten who won that 400-meter dash. But those who saw Derek Redmond finish his race will remember it forever.

Why? Because he didn't give up. No one would have blamed Derek for stopping after the fall, but he kept going.

These are letters of direction and encouragement in the faith.

Derek came to the Olympics with a single goal in mind. He saw the finish line. He had something to strive for. And he went for it, no matter what.

Goals make it possible to reach otherwise-unattainable heights. They allow you to push through obstacles that might ordinarily cause you to throw in the towel. Having a goal, a vision, is necessary for life (Proverbs 29:18).

And you have proven to have vision. Over the course of this year, you've faithfully read the Bible and pushed through this devotional. Now you head to your last lap — the General Epistles.

Like the Pauline Epistles, these are letters of direction and encouragement in the faith. Unlike the Pauline Epistles, the General Epistles have been written by a variety of different authors. Also, with the exceptions of Hebrews and Revelation, these letters are named based on authorship (rather than recipient, as Paul's are).

So let's get started. The finish line is in sight. On your mark, get set ... GO!

> **Scripture Coverage:** Hebrews – Revelation
> **Scripture Reading:** Hebrews – Revelation
> **Book Genre:** Epistles
> **Main Theme:** Letters from early Christian leaders
> to encourage and instruct in the faith
> **Main Events:** See the general description of each book
> **Main Characters:** Jesus

Note: Like November, this section will focus on the reading rather than on answering questions.

Before you read each Epistle, ask God to speak to you through His Word. As you read, consider how each book lines up with its summary below.

Week 1: Hebrews and James
Scripture: Hebrews; James

<u>Hebrews</u>: Strengthens the faith of Jewish Christians undergoing persecution, and encourages them cling to Christ without looking back.

<u>James</u>: Discusses living the Christian faith in everyday life.

Week 2: Peter and John
Scripture: 1 Peter; 2 Peter; 1 John; 2 John; 3 John

<u>1 Peter</u>: Gives an eternal perspective on life on earth in light of trials and suffering.

<u>2 Peter</u>: Exhorts believers to godliness, and exposes false prophets and teachers.

<u>1 John</u>: Exposes false teachers, and exhorts fellowship with God.

<u>2 John</u>: Urges the "chosen lady" to beware of extending hospitality to those who no longer teach the truth.

<u>3 John</u>: Offers commendation to Gaius, and warns against Diotrephes.

Week 3: Jude and Revelation
Scripture: Jude; Revelation

<u>Jude</u>: Urges believers to contend for the faith, and warns against ungodly living and false teachers.

<u>Revelation</u>: Rebukes seven churches for their compromise and sin, calls them to repentance, and provides a prophetic look into the end-times.

Week 4: Review

Review the past 12 months. Try to recount the story of the Bible from Creation to Revelation. Then write your brief summary. No more than one page should be necessary. Be sure to include the main theme: salvation through Jesus Christ.

Summary of the Bible Story

Monthly Reflection
How did this month's study help you ...

1. Understand the Bible as a continuous story?

2. See God's salvation plan for man?

3. Learn how to study the Bible?

4. Grow in your personal walk with Jesus?

The Finish Line

Congratulations! You've finished a yearlong race. May your relationship with God and your understanding of His Word continue to be blessed and grow. And, as Paul writes in 2 Timothy 4:7, may you be able to say, "I have fought the good fight, I have finished the race, I have kept the faith."

RESOURCES

Pre-Devotional Questionnaire

Answer each question on a scale of 0-10.
(0 being not at all and 10 being perfection.)

1. _____ Your understanding of the Old Testament.

2. _____ Your understanding of the New Testament.

3. _____ Your ability to relate the story of the Bible from Genesis to Revelation.

4. _____ How well can you explain God's salvation plan for man?

5. _____ Could you point out Old Testament Scripture that leads to the promise of a coming Messiah?

6. _____ How well do you understand the Biblical history of the Israelite nation?

7. _____ When you sit down to read the Bible, how well do you understand it?

8. _____ Rate your personal Bible study habits.

9. _____ Rate your personal prayer habits.

10. _____ Rate your personal relationship God (based on how close you are with Him).

Post-Devotional Questionnaire

Answer each question on a scale of 0-10.
(0 being not at all, and 10 being absolutely, yes!)

1. _____ Did you enjoy taking this study?

2. _____ Was it effective in helping you grow in your relationship with God?

3. _____ Do you have a <u>better</u> understanding of the "story of God"?

4. _____ Do you have a <u>better</u> understanding of God's salvation plan for man?

5. _____ Has this study helped you improve your personal study habits of God's Word?

6. Would you recommend this study to a friend? Why?

   _____

   _____

   _____

7. About how many hours a week did you spend on this study?

   _____

   _____

   _____

8. What did you like best about the study?

   _____

   _____

   _____

9. What suggestion would you offer to make the study better?

   _____

   _____

   _____

GLOSSARY

(1)   Testament — "covenant" or "promise"

(2)   Ordained — In this particular instance; destined or designed it to happen

(3)   Protevangelium — "pre-gospel" refers to Genesis 3:15 in which we get the first glimpse of the promise of a coming Messiah

(4)   Patriarch — The male head of a family or lineage

(5)   Providence — The manifestation of God directing the affairs of humankind by indirect means

(6)   Exodus — Going out or departure, usually of a large number of people

(7)   Omnipotence — All powerful

(8)   Law — Translation of the Hebrew word "Torah", meaning instruction or direction

(9)   Prophet — Someone who is able to hear messages from God, usually depicting what will happen in the future, and share that with the people and is accurate 100% of the time

(10)   Theophany — A manifestation of God in a visible form to man

(11)   Ephod — Sacred vestment worn by priest. Usually a linen garment made up of two pieces which was hung from the neck and covered the back and front

(12)   Nazirite — Someone who is set apart and dedicated wholly to the Lord for either a specific time or their entire life

(13)   Theocracy — a form of government in which God is the ruler

(14)   Divination — the practice of attempting to foretell future events or discover hidden knowledge by occult or supernatural means

(15)   Penitent — Expressing sorrow for sin and inclined to seek atonement

(16)   Exile — To be banished from one's native land

(17)   Pagan — A person who is not a Christian

(18)   Israel — Referring to the 10 tribes that make up the Northern part of the nation of Israel; (18b) Judah — Referring to the 2 tribes that make up the Southern part of the nation of Israel; (18c) Assyria — A warlike nation known for its brutality; (18d) Edom — A nation descended from the lineage of Esau, Jacob's brother; (18e) Babylonia — Foreign nation that Jerusalem and their inhabitants become captive to; (18f) Jerusalem — Capital city of Jerusalem.

(19)   Locust — Type of grasshopper that migrate in swarms and strips vegetation from large areas

(20)   Messiah — Title for Jesus, refers to his role as promised deliverer of Jewish people

(21) Tithe — The giving of 1/10 of our income to the Lord

(22) Parallelism — Words of two or more lines of text are directly related

(23) Figure of Speech — Using words to create a visual image

(24) Lament — to feel, show, or express grief, sorrow, or regret

(25) Proverb — Short, compact saying from God that expresses a principle on human behavior

(26) Messianic — Refers to the promise of the coming Messiah, Jesus

(27) Christ — literally means "anointed" for the redemptive work of God for man. Referring to Jesus.

(28) Gospel — "good news", message of Christianity

(29) Incarnate — Jesus taking on human flesh and coming as a man

(30) Resurrection — rising from the dead

(31) Disciples — Followers of Christ, who in this case refers to the 12 men Jesus chose to follow him

(32) Divine — Power and nature of God

(33) Sovereign — Ruler with supreme power and authority

(34) Pentecost — 2nd Festival of the Jewish year when the first fruits of harvest are presented to God

(35) Gentile — All people with the exception of the Jews

(36) Epistle — A letter written to an individual, church, or Christian body as a whole

(37) Legalism — Strict adherence to the letter of the law, rather than to the spirit of the law

ABOUT THE AUTHORS

Rev. Craig Bellisario

Craig received Christ as a college student when a high school friend shared the Good News with him. He took his newfound faith and bachelor's degree in Education from the University of Massachusetts, Amherst and taught at New Covenant Christian School for 15 years. Craig left the classroom and served as principal for several years before being called into pastoral ministry. Craig now serves as the Care and Counseling pastor of First Assembly of God in Worcester, MA. At his side is his wife, Amanda of four years and their daughter, Juliette. Craig enjoys golf, teaching the Word, and fantasy football.

Rev. Brian Minnich

Brian was completing a bachelor of science degree in Geography at Penn State University when God called him to missions through OneHope. He traveled the former Soviet Union for three years providing God's Word to children and youth, during which time his own hunger for God's Word was growing. Since then, Brian has ministered to students as both youth pastor and intern director and obtained a Master of Divinity from Gordon-Conwell Theological Seminary. Brian is currently the lead pastor of First Assembly of God in Worcester, MA and is pursuing a Doctorate in Education through Northeastern University in Boston. Together with his wife Glorieann, they are raising four great kids. As a family, they enjoy campfires, sports, comedy and seeing people's lives changed through the Word.